Quiz Wizard

Movie
Trivia

Marsha Kranes, Fred Worth & Steve Tamerius
Edited by Michael Driscoll

THE
POPULAR
GROUP

This edition published in 2001 by Popular Publishing, LLC

Copyright © 1981, 1982, 1983, 1984, 1985, 1986, 1987, 1988, 1989,
1990, 1991, 1992, 1993, 1994, 1996, 1997, 1998 by Workman.

Popular Publishing Company
3 Park Avenue
New York, NY 10016

Cover art by Eileen Toohey

Cover and interior design by Tony Meisel

Manufactured in the United States of America

ISBN 1-59027-028-2

10 9 8 7 6 5 4 3 2 1

Questions

1. What well-known Tasmanian-born leading lady launched her entertainment career under the name Queenie O'Brien?

2. In what country was famous French actor Yves Montand born?

3. What were the real first names of Beau Brummell and Beau Geste?

4. What famous character actor prepared for a career in psychiatry—studying and working with pioneer psychoanalysts Sigmund Freud and Alfred Adler—before he turned to performing?

5. In a charity pantomime performance in 1984, rocker Elton John was featured as "Mother Goose." Who co-starred as the "Egg Yolk"?

6. Bob Hope and Bing Crosby took movie "roads" to seven destinations. How many can you name?

7. Who wrote the scripts for his own films under pseudonyms that included Otis T. Criblecoblis and Mahatma Kane Jeeves?

Answers

1. Merle Oberon. Born Estelle Merle O'Brien Thompson, she went on to use a variation of her middle names for her professional name.

2. In Italy, as Yvo Livi.

3. Brummell was George; Geste, Michael.

4. Peter Lorre.

5. Sir John Gielgud.

6. Singapore, Zanzibar, Morocco, Utopia, Rio, Bali, and Hong Kong.

7. W.C. Fields.

8. What actor—and one-time New York Yankee batboy—portrayed Babe Ruth in the 1948 movie biography of the Sultan of Swat?

9. What actor's profile was once compared to "the steely prehensile outline of an invariably victorious bottle opener"?

10. Who provided Mickey Mouse's high-pitched voice in the early Walt Disney films starring the animated mouse?

11. For what two films did Elizabeth Taylor win best actress Oscars?

12. Who dubbed Miss Piggy's singing voice in *The Muppet Movie?*

13. When British film companies buy a product called Kensington Gore, what are they purchasing?

14. What American actress once described herself as "pure as the driven slush"?

15. What was the name of the popular Broadway musical that was turned into the 1934 movie *The Gay Divorcée?*

16. Who said: "A man in love is incomplete until he is married. Then he is finished"?

8. William Bendix.

9. George C. Scott's. Critic Kenneth Tynan made the comparison.

10. Walt Disney, himself.

11. Butterfield 8, *in 1960;* Who's Afraid of Virginia Woolf, *in 1966.*

12. Johnny Matthis.

13. Artificial blood, used for special effects.

14. Tallulah Bankhead.

15. The Gay Divorce. *The Hollywood censors nixed that title, however, apparently finding it inappropriate to call a divorce happy.*

16. Oft-married Zsa Zsa Gabor.

17. What film did Ingrid Bergman make twice—first in Swedish and then in English for her Hollywood debut?

18. What was the only horror film in which Humphrey Bogart appeared?

19. What color was actor Yul Brynner's hair—when he had hair?

20. Who was Gene Kelly's unusual dancing partner in an imaginative pas de deux in the 1945 film *Anchors Aweigh?*

21. What entertainer boxed under the name Kid Crochet as a teenager?

22. How old was Shirley Temple when she appeared in her first film, *The Red-Haired Alibi?*

23. For what offense was Australian-born *Million Dollar Mermaid* Annette Kellerman, the first aquatic glamour girl, arrested in 1909?

24. Who played Scorpio, the sadistic killer, in Clint Eastwood's 1971 film, *Dirty Harry?*

25. What British actor made his screen debut as a Mexican wearing a blanket in the very first Hopalong Cassidy movie?

17. Intermezzo: A Love Story.

18. The Return of Dr. X. *Bogart played a zombie in the 1939 film.*

19. Dark brown.

20. Jerry, the animated mouse from the Tom and Jerry *cartoon.*

21.Dean Martin, was born Dino Crocetti.

22. Three years old.

23. Indecent exposure—for wearing one of her newly created, one-piece bathing suits. The skirtless creation covered her legs all the way down to the calf.

24. Andy Robinson, son of Edward G. Robinson.

25. David Niven, who noted, "Of course they daren't let me open my mouth."

26. Who wrote the screenplay for *The Misfits,* the 1961 film that marked the last screen appearances of both Clark Gable and Marilyn Monroe?

27. What 1977 movie was originally going to be called *Anhedonia*—a word that means the psychological inability to experience pleasure?

28. Whose lengthy Oscar acceptance speech prompted the Academy of Motion Picture Arts and Sciences to set a time limit at later award ceremonies?

29. What was the name of the dolphin that played Flipper in the movies?

30. What famous American actress made her stage debut in 1966 as a silent Helen of Troy in *Dr. Faustus?*

31. In what film did tough guy actor Clint Eastwood first deliver his trademark line, "Make my day"?

32. What was the first R-rated film produced by the Walt Disney studio?

33. What was used to simulate blood in the famous shower scene in the 1960 Alfred Hitchcock chiller *Psycho?*

34. Comedian W.C. Fields' waterfront summer home in New York City was sold in 1980 so that an existing business could expand. What was the business?

26. Monroe's ex-husband, Pulitzer Prize–winning playwright Arthur Miller.

27. Woody Allen's Annie Hall.

28. Greer Garson's. She said her thanks for 5 1/2 minutes at the 1943 ceremonies when she was honored for her starring role in Mrs. Miniver.

29. Mitzi. For the TV series she was replaced by two other dolphins, Suzy and Cathy.

30. Elizabeth Taylor. Her first speaking role in the theater came 15 years later when she appeared on Broadway in Lillian Hellman's The Little Foxes.

31. In Sudden Impact, *during his fourth appearance as Inspector "Dirty Harry" Callahan.*

32. Down and Out in Beverly Hills, *starring Richard Dreyfuss, Bette Midler and Nick Nolte, in 1985.*

33.Hershey's chocolate syrup.

34. The home of the man who reportedly once said, "Any man who hates children and dogs can't be all bad," was purchased by a nursery school.

35. In the 1952 hit musical *Singin' in the Rain*, who dubbed the splash dancing heard while Gene Kelly does his celebrated tap dance in the rain?

36. What do Rudolf Nureyev's legs, Bette Davis's waistline and Jimmy Durante's nose have in common?

37. What song was the musical theme of James Cagney's 1931 gangster classic *Public Enemy*?

38. What great American actor's first stage appearance was as a chorus girl in a show called *Every Sailor*?

39. What was Boris Karloff's real name?

40. What was the real name of the elderly British schoolteacher in the James Hilton novel *Goodbye, Mr. Chips,* portrayed on the silver screen by Robert Donat?

41. What famous Hollywood leading man appeared as Pinkerton in the 1932 non-musical film version of the Giacomo Puccini opera *Madame Butterfly?*

42. Actresses Mary Pickford and Alexis Smith were both born with the same name—and changed it for Hollywood. What was it?

43. How many costume changes did Elizabeth Taylor make in the $37 million, 1963 motion picture extravaganza *Cleopatra?*

44. What were the first words spoken by Greta Garbo in a movie?

35. *Then-unknowns Gwen Verdon and Carol Haney.*

36. *All were insured by Lloyd's of London.*

37. *"I'm Forever Blowing Bubbles."*

38. *James Cagney's, in 1920.*

39. *William Henry Pratt.*

40. *Mr. Chipping.*

41. *Cary Grant. Sylvia Sidney was his Madame Butterfly.*

42. *Gladys Smith.*

43. *Sixty-five.*

44. *"Gimme a vhiskey. Ginger ale on the side. An' don' be stingy, baby." The film was* Anna Christie; *the year, 1930.*

45. What unusual pet did actor John Barrymore have?

46. What 1939 James Stewart movie classic aroused Congressional threats against Hollywood and attempts to block its European release by U.S. Ambassador to England Joseph P. Kennedy?

47. What actress changed her name from Edda van Heemstra for Hollywood?

48. What starring role did film stars Robert Redford, Steve McQueen and Paul Newman all turn down, despite a contract offer of $4 million?

49. What was the nationality of Warner Oland, the actor who appeared as Charlie Chan in dozens of films?

50. What 1935 movie was the silver screen's first Technicolor offering?

51. Who dressed in Greta Garbo's clothes and doubled for her in a horseback-riding scene in her first American movie, the 1926 silent film *Torrent?*

52. In the 1968 film *2001: A Space Odyssey,* what song did HAL, the computer, learn to sing?

53. Who dubbed the voice of Darth Vader in the movies *Star Wars* and *The Empire Strikes Back?*

45. *A vulture named Maloney. It would sit on his knee and hiss.*

46. *Frank Capra's* Mr. Smith Goes To Washington.

47. *Belgian-born Audrey Hepburn.*

48. Superman. *Christopher Reeve took the part—for* $250,000.

49. *He was Swedish.*

50. Becky Sharp, *a film adaptation of the William Makepeace Thackeray novel* Vanity Fair.

51. *Actor Joel McCrea.*

52. *"A Bicycle Built For Two."*

53. *James Earl Jones.*

54. What was the name of the Good Witch portrayed by Billie Burke in the 1939 film classic *The Wizard of Oz?*

55. Who was Fred Astaire's first silver screen dancing partner?

56. What was the name of the mechanical shark in the 1975 hit movie *Jaws?*

57. What 1960 film classic is based on the Edward Gein murder case?

58. What famous American playwright wrote the script for *The Cocoanuts* and several other Marx Brothers movies?

59. What American actress was the first to have a theater named after her?

60. What unusual insurance policy did silent-film slapstick comedian Ben Turpin take out?

61. For starring roles in what two films did Jane Fonda win Oscars?

62. Who played Vincent Price's menacing mute assistant in the 3-D horror film *House of Wax?*

63. What Oscar-winning 1971 movie was based on the 1951 Broadway play *I Am a Camera?*

54. Glinda.

55. Joan Crawford, in Dancing Lady *in 1933. Later that year he teamed up with Ginger Rogers in* Flying Down to Rio.

56. Bruce.

57. Alfred Hitchcock's Psycho.

58. George S. Kaufman.

59. Ethel Barrymore. The theater, in New York, opened in 1928.

60. A $100,000 policy against the possibility that his trademark crossed eyes would straighten out.

61. Klute, *in 1971, and* Coming Home, *in 1978.*

62. Charles Bronson, in 1953, before he changed his name from Charles Buchinski.

63. Cabaret, *starring Liza Minnelli and Joel Grey.*

64. Robert Redford was paid $6 million for his role in the 1985 film *Out of Africa*. How much was leading lady Meryl Streep paid?

65. A process called Smell-O-Vision was used in 1960 for one film and then abandoned forever. What was the odorous offering?

66. How did Charlie Chaplin place when he entered a Charlie Chaplin lookalike contest in Monte Carlo?

67. What movie's cast included 124 midgets?

68. What movie series did Johnny Weissmuller star in after he outgrew his "Tarzan" loincloth?

69. Who replaced Dorothy Lamour as the female lead in the last of the seven Bing Crosby-Bob Hope "Road" movies?

70. What famous American movie star's ashes are in an urn that also contains a small gold whistle?

71. Rudolph Valentino, the great lover, was married twice. How did he spend his wedding nights?

72. What film star represented Scotland in the 1952 Mr. Universe contest?

73. What was movie mogul Samuel Goldwyn's real name?

64. She received $3 million.

65. Scent of Mystery, *produced by Mike Todd, Jr.*

66. He came in third.

67. The 1939 version of The Wizard of Oz, *starring Judy Garland. The midgets played Munchkins.*

68. Jungle Jim, *in which he wore a bush jacket to cover his added weight.*

69. Joan Collins. Lamour, however, did make a cameo appearance in the 1962 film, The Road to Hong Kong.

70. Humphrey Bogart's. His actress wife Lauren Bacall had the whistle inscribed, "If you need anything, just whistle"—words she spoke to him in their first film together, To Have and Have Not.

71. His first, locked out by wife Jean Acker; his second, in jail for bigamy, unable to be with wife Natacha Rambova.

72. Sean Connery.

73. Samuel Goldfish. He took his new name from the company he formed with the Selwyn brothers.

74. How much was Marlon Brando paid for his brief appearance as Jor-el in the movie *Superman?*

75. What is Dolly Parton's CB "handle"?

76. What actress in what movie said, "How dare he make love to me and not be a married man"?

77. How much does the 13 $\frac{1}{2}$-inch-tall Academy Award Oscar weigh?

78. What famous passenger ship was sunk to provide the dramatic climax of the 1960 film, *The Last Voyage?*

79. What actor claims he is never without his emerald-green socks?

80. Can you name the three boxers Sylvester Stallone faced in the climactic scenes of his first four *Rocky* movies?

81. What actress was the granddaughter of famed architect Frank Lloyd Wright?

82. Who dubbed Lauren Bacall's singing voice in *To Have and Have Not*, her screen debut and first pairing with future husband Humphrey Bogart?

83. In what three films did Doris Day sing "Que Sera Sera"?

84. What two film classics did Victor Fleming direct in 1939?

74. He received a reported $3.7 million, as well as another $15 million after suing for a share of the box-office take.

75. Booby Trap.

76. Ingrid Berman, speaking of Cary Grant in Indiscreet.

77. The statuette weighs eight and a half pounds.

78. The Ile de France, *which was renamed* Faransu Maru *("French Ship" in Japanese) for the occasion.*

79. Irish-born Peter O'Toole.

80. Apollo Creed (Carl Weathers) in Rocky *and* Rocky II; *Clubber Lang (Mr. T) in* Rocky III; *and Drago (Dolph Ludgren) in* Rocky IV.

81. Anne Baxter.

82. A teenage Andy Williams.

83. The Man Who Knew Too Much *in 1956;* Please Don't Eat the Daisies *in 1960; and* The Glass Bottom Boat *in 1966.*

84. Gone With the Wind *and* The Wizard of Oz.

85. In what film did the star propose by saying, "Marry me and I'll never look at another horse"?

86. What screen role did Telly Savalas, Donald Pleasance, Max Von Sydow and Charles Gray have in common?

87. For her role of Rosie in the 1951 film classic *The African Queen*, who was Katharine Hepburn told to use as a model?

88. In what film classic was the heroine advised: "You can't show your bosom 'fore three o'clock"?

89. What was the first British sound film?

90. What comedienne is a direct descendant of Edward Rutledge, the youngest signer of the Declaration of Independence?

91. At an MGM auction in 1970, two items went for the top price of $1,500. One was the full-sized boat used in the musical *Showboat*. What was the other?

92. Clark Gable starred in the 1932 film *Red Dust* with Jean Harlow and Mary Astor. What was the name of the 1953 remake, featuring Gable in the same role with costars Ava Gardner and Grace Kelly?

93. What filmmaker made a cameo appearance in *Close Encounters of the Third Kind?*

85. A Day at the Races. *Groucho Marx was popping the question to Margaret Dumont.*

86. *All played SPECTRE chief Ernst Stavro Blofeld in James Bond films.*

87. *Eleanor Roosevelt.*

88. Gone With the Wind. *Hattie McDaniels gave the etiquette tip to Vivien Leigh.*

89. Blackmail, *Alfred Hitchcock's 1929 masterpiece.*

90. *Goldie Hawn.*

91. *Judy Garland's size-4 $\frac{1}{2}$ red shoes from* The Wizard of Oz.

92. Mogambo.

93. *François Truffaut. He appeared as a UFO expert.*

94. What famous actor starred in two classic "Bridge" movies?

95. Who appeared as a character named Alias in the 1973 Sam Peckinpah film *Pat Garrett and Billy the Kid?*

96. What famous performer appeared in a movie riding Trigger before Roy Rogers rode him to silver-screen stardom?

97. Who subbed for Claire Bloom in the dance sequences in the 1952 film *Limelight,* which also starred Charlie Chaplin?

98. Who portrayed Snow White in a live-action movie to help Walt Disney's animators achieve realism in their cartoon feature film?

99. What actress once sued a California animal breeder for naming a two-headed goat after her?

100. Who was William Claude Dukenfield?

101. What film did Alfred Hitchcock make twice?

102. Where were the disco scenes in *Saturday Night Fever* shot?

103. Who played "The Great Gatsby" in the 1949 film version of the F. Scott Fitzgerald novel?

94. William Holden. He was in The Bridge on the River Kwai *and* The Bridges at Toko-ri.

95. Singer Bob Dylan.

96. Olivia de Havilland, in The Adventures of Robin Hood *in 1938. At the time, Trigger was known as Golden Cloud.*

97. Ballerina Melissa Hayden.

98. Dancer Marge Champion, who was married to a Disney animator at the time. She also was the model for the Blue Fairy in Pinocchio.

99. Hedy Lamarr.

100. Comedian W.C. Fields.

101. The Man Who Knew Too Much—*in 1934 with Leslie Banks and Edna Best, and in 1956 with James Stewart and Doris Day.*

102. At the 2001 Odyssey Disco in Bay Ridge, Brooklyn.

103. Alan Ladd. Robert Redford starred in the same role 25 years later.

104. What film star won a special Oscar as "the most outstanding personality of 1934"?

105. What actor launched his performing career as a public-address announcer for the Brooklyn Dodgers at Ebbets Field in 1938?

106. In his first starring role in the 1935 film *The Phantom Empire*, what horse did Gene Autry ride?

107. In what film did the heroine declare, "I've met the most wonderful man. Of course, he's fictional. But you can't have everything"?

108. Who launched her film career at age 10 in a low-brow comedy called *There's One Born Every Minute*, which also featured former Our Gang star Carl "Alfalfa" Switzer?

109. In the Walk Disney film, what was the profession of Snow White's friends, the seven dwarfs?

110. Who paid $300 for 32 cotton sheets and 35 pillow cases—worth $50 new—at an auction of actor John Gilbert's personal effects following his death in 1936?

111. Who was scheduled to star in the 1984 film *Beverly Hills Cop* before the role went to Eddie Murphy?

112. Which of his almost 100 movies was Roy Rogers' favorite?

104. America's dimpled darling Shirley Temple, who was Hollywood's top box-office attraction from 1935 through 1938.

105. John Forsythe.

106. Tom Mix's horse Tony Jr.—not Champion.

107. The Purple Rose of Cairo, *starring Mia Farrow.*

108. Elizabeth Taylor.

109. Bashful, Doc, Dopey, Grumpy, Happy, Sleepy and Sneezy were jewel miners.

110. Marlene Dietrich.

111. Sylvester Stallone, in a much more macho version written by Rocky-Rambo himself. And before Stallone, Mickey Rourke had been slated for the part.

112. My Pal Trigger.

113. For which Alfred Hitchcock film did artist Salvadore Dali design the graphics?

114. Which profile did actor John Barrymore consider "the moneymaking side" of his face?

115. What famous American author appeared in the 1976 movie comedy *Murder by Death*?

116. In Walt Disney's 1938 cartoon short *Mother Goose Goes Hollywood*, what star was caricaturized as Little Bo-Peep?

117. Who starred in the title role in the 1977 film *Valentino*?

118. Two movies were named after the song "Red River Valley." Who starred in them?

119. Who said, "If I had as many love affairs as you have given me credit for, I would now be speaking to you from a jar in the Harvard Medical School"?

120. When Eddie Cantor ducks to avoid a handful of mud in the 1932 film *Roman Scandals*, what Goldwyn girl gets it right in the face?

121. Who coined the phrase "cameo role" to describe the appearance of a top movie star in a bit part?

122. In what film did Jean Arthur make her last screen appearance?

113. Spellbound, *in 1945. Dali created the graphics for amnesiac Gregory Peck's Freudian dreams.*

114. *The left.*

115. *Truman Capote.*

116. *Katherine Hepburn.*

117. *Another Rudolph—Rudolf Nureyev.*

118. *Gene Autry in 1936; Roy Rogers in 1941. The song originated in New York at the turn of the century as "In the Bright Mohawk Valley."*

119. *Frank Sinatra.*

120. *Lucille Ball.*

121. *Showman Mike Todd, when he produced his Oscar-winning* Around the World in 80 Days *in 1955. It featured Frank Sinatra, Marlene Dietrich, Buster Keaton, Noel Coward, Ronald Colman, Beatrice Lillie and others in unexpected walk-ons.*

122. *In* Shane, *in 1953.*

123. What Hollywood movie star's contract included a morals clause that forbade "adulterous conduct or immoral relations" with men other than her husband?

124. Paul Newman took an ad in a newspaper to apologize for what movie, when the film was shown on TV?

125. Whom did Fred Astaire name as his favorite dance partner?

126. What American film classic did actor John Wayne call "the most un-American thing I've ever seen in my whole life"?

127. Whom did actor Richard Dreyfuss portray in his first important film role—in the 1973 movie *Dillinger?*

128. How old was actress Joan Collins when she posed semi-nude for Playboy in 1983?

129. Italian film producer Carlo Ponti was considered for the title role of what 1972 blockbuster movie?

130. Who played Watergate cover-up informant Deep Throat in the 1976 film *All The President's Men?*

131. What struggling movie cowboy served as Gary Cooper's dialogue coach for his first all-talkie, the 1929 western classic *The Virginian?*

123. Gloria Swanson's.

124. His 1954 screen debut, The Silver Chalice.

125. Gene Kelly.

126. The 1952 Gary Cooper western High Noon. *Wayne's objection: "The last thing in the picture is ole Coop putting the United States marshal's badge under his foot and stepping on it."*

127. George "Baby Face" Nelson. Warren Oates was featured in the title role.

128. 50. The issue sold out.

129. The Godfather. *Marlon Brando, the actor who finally got the role of Don Vito Corleone, won an Oscar for his performance.*

130. Hal Holbrook.

131. Randolph Scott. Scott, a native Virginian, had a bit part in the film.

132. What did actor Jack Lemmon use to strain spaghetti in the 1960 comedy classic *The Apartment?*

133. What 1959 film ends with the heroine saying, "In spite of everything, I still believe that people are good at heart"?

134. Actor Peter Fonda was once arrested and charged with disturbing the peace and destroying private property for slashing a sign. What did the sign say?

135. What was the name of actress Elizabeth Taylor's childhood pet chipmunk, which she immortalized in a book written in 1946?

136. A life-size statue of what Hollywood filmmaker has been erected in Puerto Vallarta, Mexico?

137. What two tough-guy actors turned down the role of the avenging "Man with No Name" in Sergio Leone's spaghetti western *A Fistful of Dollars* before Clint Eastwood was offered the part?

138. What popular movie was remade in 1981 under the title *Outland,* with Sean Connery in the lead role and the setting shifted from the Old West to the third moon of Jupiter?

139. How many frames per second are projected in most animated films?

140. Who dubbed the voice of the Beast in the animated 1991 Disney version of *Beauty and the Beast?*

132. A tennis racquet.

133. The Diary of Anne Frank.

134. "Feed Jane Fonda to the Whales." Charges against Fonda were dropped when two key witnesses to the 1981 incident at Denver's Stapleton International Airport failed to appear at his trial.

135. Nibbles. Taylor wrote and illustrated the book Nibbles and Me when she was 14.

136. Director John Huston—because of the number of tourists drawn to the picturesque seaside village by his 1964 hit The Night of the Iguana.

137. James Coburn and Charles Bronson. Henry Fonda was the first choice, but he was too expensive.

138. High Noon.

139. 24.

140. Robby Benson.

141. What famous actor's brother enjoyed a brief movie career as a child, appearing in a bit part in the 1939 Frank Capra classic *Mr. Smith Goes to Washington*?

142. What was the name of the stray alley cat adopted by Holly Golightly, portrayed by Audrey Hepburn, in the 1961 movie *Breakfast at Tiffany's*?

143. What 1977 R-rated hit movie was later re-released with a PG rating after seven minutes of footage had been removed?

144. What was the first name of Lt. Bullitt, the down-and-dirty San Francisco detective portrayed by Steve McQueen in the 1968 hit movie *Bullitt*?

145. In what year did Hollywood start keeping the names of Oscar winners sealed and secret?

146. What unusual message did actress Joan Hackett have inscribed on her grave marker?

147. In what roles did Francis Ford Coppola's daughter, Sofia, appear in each of the Godfather movies?

148. Which is the only airline "Rain Man" Dustin Hoffman says he would be willing to fly in the 1988 Academy Award-winning film?

149. Under what pseudonym did strongman Arnold Schwarzenegger make his screen debut?

141. Dustin Hoffman's older brother Ronald.

142. It had no name—she called it "cat."

143. Saturday Night Fever, *starring John Travolta. The cut footage featured some sex scenes and blue language.*

144. Frank.

145. 1940—the year after the Los Angeles Times broke its promise and published the names of the winners before they had been officially announced.

146. "Go Away! I'm Sleeping."

147. In The Godfather *she was a baby; in* The Godfather, Part II, *she was a child immigrant; and in* The Godfather, Part III, *in her first speaking part, she played Godfather Michael Corleone's daughter, Mary.*

148. Qantas, because of its safety record.

149. Arnold Strong. He starred in the 1970 Italian-TV film Hercules in New York.

150. Who wrote the 1975 Academy Award-winning song "I'm Easy" for the movie Nashville?

151. What is comedian Chevy Chase's real first name?

152. What movie star's trademark telephone greeting became the title of a popular 1965 movie comedy?

153. What Cecil B. deMille film was the first movie to include screen credits?

154. By what name do we know the play and cult movie that was originally going to be called *They Came From Denton High*?

155. What were the names of mad scientist Dr. Emmett Brown's dogs in *Back to the Future* and *Back to the Future II*?

156. Who wrote and directed the 1984 "rockumentary" satire *This Is Spinal Tap* and the 1986 hit *Stand By Me*?

157. In the 1953 film *Mogambo*, what did Clark Gable reply when Grace Kelly asked, "Who is this man Thomson that gazelles should be called after him?"

158. Who were the only consecutive Best Actress Oscar winners to appear together in the first movie both made after receiving their awards?

159. What movie introduced the song "Some Day My Prince Will Come"?

150. Actor Keith Carradine, who sang the song in the film and at the Oscar ceremonies.

151. Cornelius.

152. Warren Beatty's line "What's new, pussycat."

153. His 1913 silent version of Squaw Man—*the first of three versions deMille made of the story.*

154. The Rocky Horror Picture Show.

155. Einstein and Copernicus.

156. Rob Reiner, who once played Mike "Meathead" Stivic on TV's All in the Family.

157. Gable said: "He's a third baseman for the Giants who got a home run against the Dodgers once." Actually, the Thomson's gazelle is named for 19th-century Scottish explorer Joseph Thomson, who was the first European to visit many regions of East Africa.

158. Jessica Tandy, who won the Oscar in 1989 for Driving Miss Daisy, *and Kathy Bates, who won it in 1990 for* Misery. *Their joint project was the 1992 film* Fried Green Tomatoes.

159. Walt Disney's 1937 Snow White and the Seven Dwarfs. *The song was written for the film by Frank Churchill and Larry Morey.*

160. What film star early in his career appeared in a series of movies as Singin' Sam, the silver screen's first singing cowboy?

161. What Oscar-winning title role, rejected by both Marlon Brando and Albert Finney, brought stardom to the little-known actor who signed for the part?

162. What was the name of Baby Jane's wheelchair-bound sister in the 1962 chiller *Whatever Happened to Baby Jane?*, starring Bette Davis and Joan Crawford?

163. What four 1939 Hollywood classics were honored on 25-cent stamps issued by the U.S. Postal Service in celebration of their 50th anniversaries?

164. What movie star couple, in a bid to discourage sightseers, once put a hand-painted sign in front of their Beverly Hills home that said "Please—They have Moved!—The Piersons"?

165. Who appeared as God in the 1968 Otto Preminger film *Skidoo?*

166. According to his Nazi dossier in the 1942 film classic Casablanca, what color are Rick's eyes?

167. Who turned down the role of Bonnie in the 1967 hit movie *Bonnie and Clyde* before Faye Dunaway got the part?

160. John Wayne. He gave up the role because his singing and guitar-playing were dubbed, making personal appearances difficult if not impossible.

161. Lawrence of Arabia. *The role, of course, went to Peter O'Toole.*

162. Blanche. Davis played Jane; Crawford, Blanche.

163. Gone With the Wind, Beau Geste, Stagecoach *and* The Wizard of Oz.

164. Paul Newman and Joanne Woodward.

165. Groucho Marx.

166. Brown. In the film, Rick—played by brown-eyed Humphrey Bogart—asks Major Strasser, "Are my eyes really brown?" when he's handed a copy of his dossier.

167. Jane Fonda.

168. What unique money-saving attachments did Greta Garbo have installed in her Duesenberg automobile?

169. How many films had Humphrey Bogart made when he co-starred with wife-to-be Lauren Bacall in her first movie, *To Have and Have Not*, in 1945?

170. Who played the parole officer of elderly ex-con train robbers Burt Lancaster and Kirk Douglas in the 1986 film comedy *Tough Guys?*

171. Why has actor Robert Duvall named several of his pet dogs Boo Radley?

172. What 1987 chiller was an expanded version of a 45-minute 1979 British film called *Diversion?*

173. What line, delivered by Carole Lombard to William Powell in the 1936 comedy *My Man Godfrey*, inspired the trademark greeting of a popular cartoon character?

174. What actress, asked to audition for a supporting role in a 1990 Hollywood movie, sat down at the casting director's desk, pulled two Oscars from a satchel and demanded, "Do you still want me to read for this part?"

175. Who was listed as "Shakespearean Tutor to Mr. Newman" in the credits for the 1990 Paul Newman—Joanne Woodward film *Mr. and Mrs. Bridge?*

168. Safes—six of them.

169. 50.

170. Comedian Dana Carvey, best known as the Church Lady on TV's Saturday Night Live, and as Garth Algar in the 1992 film Wayne's World.

171. In honor of his breakthrough film role as Boo Radley, the reclusive, retarded neighbor in the 1962 movie To Kill a Mockingbird.

172. Fatal Attraction. The screenplays of both were written by James Dearden.

173. "What's up, Duke?"—which Bugs Bunny's creator Bob Clampett borrowed and turned into "What's up, Doc?"

174. Shelley Winters. The film was Awakenings. The part she auditioned for—Robert De Niro's mother—went to actress Ruth Nelson.

175. Senator Bob Dole. Newman, who played a Kansas lawyer in the film, had asked the Kansas senator to help him get the accent right by tape-recording part of the balcony scene from Romeo and Juliet (which Newman recites in the film).

176. What did Marilyn Monroe reply when a journalist asked her what she wore to bed?

177. What famous actor worked at New York's Central Park Zoo—sweeping out the lion cages—to support himself while trying to make it in show biz?

178. What hairy covering was used to make a 40-foot-high, 6 1/2-ton mechanical ape look lifelike in the 1976 remake of the 1933 film classic *King Kong*?

179. What do the initials RKO stand for in the theater company's name?

180. In 1980, who were the Top 10 box-office stars in Hollywood, according to the nation's film exhibitors?

181. Who played Nicky Jr., son of Nick and Nora Charles, in the last of the six films in the Thin Man series, *Song of the Thin Man*?

182. Under the motion picture censorship code in effect from 1934 to 1968, how long did a screen kiss have to last to be judged "indecent"?

183. What film role did actresses Theda Bara, Claudette Colbert and Elizabeth Taylor have in common?

184. What did writer Somerset Maugham ask about Spencer Tracy's performance during a visit to the set of the 1941 film *Dr. Jekyll and Mr. Hyde*?

176. "Chanel No. 5."

177. Sylvester Stallone.

178. Argentine horse tails—2 tons of them.

179. Radio-Keith-Orpheum. It was formed by the merger of the Radio Corporation of America (RCA) and the Keith-Orpheum theater chain in 1921.

180. From 1 to 10: Burt Reynolds, Robert Redford, Clint Eastwood, Jane Fonda, Dustin Hoffman, John Travolta, Sally Field, Sissy Spacek, Barbra Streisand and Steve Martin.

181. Dean Stockwell.

182. More than thirty seconds.

183. Cleopatra. Each starred in a film entitled Cleopatra—Bara in 1917; Colbert in 1934; Taylor in 1963. Others who appeared as the Egyptian queen include Vivien Leigh, in Caesar and Cleopatra, 1945; Rhonda Fleming, in Serpent of the Nile, 1953; and Hedy Lamarr, in The Story of Mankind, 1957.

184. "Which one is he playing now?"

185. On a movie set, what is the job of the "best boy"?

186. Who was the youngest performer in history to win an Oscar?

187. What was Sleeping Beauty's name in the 1959 Walt Disney film?

188. What famous American actor made his screen debut portraying a paraplegic war veteran struggling to overcome his handicap?

189. Jack Palance portrayed Cuban dictator Fidel Castro in the 1969 movie *Che!* Who appeared in the title role as revolutionary leader Che Guevara?

190. Where did actress Sigourney Weaver—whose given name was Susan—find her unusual adopted first name?

191. What line did Jean Arthur deliver to Cary Grant in *Only Angels Have Wings* that Lauren Bacall repeated to Humphrey Bogart in *To Have and Have Not* and Angie Dickinson said to John Wayne in *Rio Bravo?*

192. Who once said, "I always wanted to do what my mother did—get all dressed up, shoot people, fall in the mud. I never considered doing anything else"?

193. Can you name Hollywood's Top 10 box-office stars of 1965—according to the nation's film exhibitors?

185. Assisting the "gaffer," or chief electrician.

186. Tatum O'Neal, who was 10 when she won an Oscar for best supporting actress as a chain-smoking, foul-mouthed young con artist in the 1973 film Paper Moon.

187. Princess Aurora. The Good Fairies, however, called her Briar Rose.

188. Marlon Brandon, in the 1950 film The Men.

189. Egyptian-born Omar Sharif.

190. In The Great Gatsby *by F. Scott Fitzgerald. Sigourney is a minor character in the book.*

191. "I'm hard to get—all you have to do is ask me." All three films were directed by Howard Hawks.

192. Actress Carrie Fisher, daughter of Debbie Reynolds.

193. From 1 to 10: Sean Connery, John Wayne, Doris Day, Julie Andrews, Jack Lemmon, Elvis Presley, Cary Grant, James Stewart, Elizabeth Taylor and Richard Burton.

194. What were the names of Bambi's rabbit and skunk friends in the 1942 Walt Disney film *Bambi?*

195. What top Hollywood star co-scripted and co-produced *Head,* a 1968 psychedelic musical fantasy that starred the rock group the Monkees?

196. By what stage names do we know father and son actors Ramon and Carlos Estevez?

197. Three stars appearing in the 1953 Academy Award-winning film *From Here to Eternity* were nominated for best actor or best actress Oscars. How many won?

198. Who won a job in Hollywood after appearing in a screen test wearing only a loincloth and sporting a rose behind his left ear?

199. Russia permitted the 1940 American film classic *The Grapes of Wrath* to be shown because of the grim picture it painted of the American depression. Why was it later banned?

200. Who played the tyrannical king in the movie *Anna and the King of Siam*—10 years before Yul Brynner starred in the musical version, *The King and I?*

201. What was the name of the hard-nosed paratrooper colonel who blasted apart a Coca-Cola vending machine in Stanley Kubrick's 1964 film satire *Dr. Strangelove?*

194. The rabbit was Thumper; the skunk, Flower.

195. Jack Nicholson.

196. Ramon is Martin Sheen; Carlos is his son Charlie Sheen. The name was inspired by Roman Catholic Bishop Fulton J. Sheen.

197. None. Burt Lancaster and Montgomery Clift lost to William Holden (Stalag 17) for best actor, and Deborah Kerr lost to Audrey Hepburn (Roman Holiday) for best actress. But Frank Sinatra won an Oscar for best supporting actor, and Donna Reed won one for best supporting actress.

198. Clark Gable.

199. Because Russian audiences were impressed that the poor, struggling Dust Bowl family depicted in the film was able to own an automobile.

200. Rex Harrison, in 1946. His co-star was Irene Dunne.

201. Bat Guano, who was portrayed by Keenan Wynn.

202. What distinguished English actor appeared as pirate William Kidd in the 1952 film *Abbott and Costello Meet Captain Kidd?*

203. Can you name the four "Lucky H" movies that actor Paul Newman starred in during the 1960s?

204. What unusual insurance policy did Anthony Quinn take out when he agreed to appear in the 1968 film *The Magus?*

205. In 1940, what Hollywood stars were voted the Top 10 box-office attractions in the land by the nation's film exhibitors?

206. What comedy team appeared in more movies than any other in U.S. film history?

207. In what film did Julie Andrews make her first appearance in a non-singing role?

208. What historic figure has been portrayed on the silver screen by actors Errol Flynn, Clark Gable, Marlon Brando and Mel Gibson?

209. Who played Mr. Smith in the 1937 Irene Dunne-Cary Grant comedy *The Awful Truth* and George in the 1938 Katherine Hepburn-Cary Grant comedy *Bringing Up Baby?*

210. What was Marion Michael Morrison's screen name before he sought stardom as John Wayne?

202. Charles Laughton.

203. The Hustler, *1961;* Hud, *1963;* Harper, *1966; and* Hombre, *1967.*

204. Quinn, who shaved his head for his role, was insured against failing to grow back a healthy head of hair.

205. From 1 to 10: Mickey Rooney, Spencer Tracy, Clark Gable, Gene Autry, Tyrone Power, James Cagney, Bing Crosby, Wallace Beery, Bette Davis and Judy Garland.

206. The Three Stooges.

207. In The Americanization of Emily, *in 1964.*

208. Fletcher Christian, first mate on the Bounty. Flynn in In the Wake of the Bounty, *in 1933; Gable in* Mutiny on the Bounty, *in 1935; Brando in* Mutiny on the Bounty, *in 1962; and Gibson in* The Bounty, *in 1984.*

209. Asta, the terrier who became a star in the Thin Man series.

210. Duke Morrison.

211. Rotund comedian Billy Gilbert, famous for his repertoire of violent sneezes, dubbed the voice of Sneezy in Walt Disney's *Snow White and the Seven Dwarfs*. Whose voice was used for Dopey in the 1937 cartoon classic?

212. What cameo role did Charlie Chaplain play in his last movie, *A Countess from Hong Kong*, in 1967?

213. What famous Hollywood star was married to Avrom Goldbogen?

214. Who appeared in the 1957 Elvis Presley film *Loving You* as members of an enthusiastic audience?

215. In the 1954 film *Her Twelve Men*, Greer Garson portrays a dedicated school teacher at a boys' school. How many boys were in her class?

216. Who were the four artists of the silver screen who founded the United Artists film company in 1919?

217. What Academy Award-winning title role was turned down by Hollywood heavy-hitters Burt Lancaster, John Wayne, Robert Mitchum, Lee Marvin and Rod Steiger?

218. Producer-director Otto Preminger paid Columbia Pictures $100,000 to use Kim Novak in the 1956 film *The Man with the Golden Arm*. How much was Novak paid?

211. No one's—Dopey was a mute in the movie.

212. He appeared as an elderly, seasick ship's steward in the film, which starred Marlon Brando and Sophia Loren.

213. Elizabeth Taylor—long after Goldbrogen had changed his name to Mike Todd.

214. Elvis' parents, Gladys and Vernon.

215. Thirteen.

216. Douglas Fairbanks, Mary Pickford, Charlie Chaplain and D.W. Griffith.

217. Patton, in 1970. George C. Scott got the role.

218. Her salary was $100 a week.

219. Why was popcorn banned at most movie theaters in the 1920s?

220. Why was Mike Nichols fired as a busboy at a Howard Johnson's restaurant in New York, where he worked while taking drama lessons in the early 1950s?

221. Under what name did a family named Blythe gain fame on stage and screen?

222. On what planet did Abbott and Costello land in their 1953 film *Abbott and Costello Go to Mars*?

223. How much were Spencer Tracy and Katharine Hepburn paid for their last joint film appearance—in the 1967 film *Guess Who's Coming to Dinner*?

224. How much was paid at a 1987 auction for Charlie Chaplin's famous bowler hat and cane?

225. What 1955 American movie was shown in Hong Kong under the title *The Heart of a Lady as Pure as a Full Moon Over the Place of Medical Salvation*?

226. What Hollywood great started his show business career on Broadway dancing in the background in Eskimo clothes as Mary Martin sang "My Heart Belongs to Daddy"?

227. What now-famous actress had a bit part as Woody Allen's date at the end of his 1977 film *Annie Hall*?

219. It was considered too noisy.

220. He claims he was canned "when somebody asked me the ice cream flavor of the week and I said, 'Chicken.'"

221. Barrymore—as in John, Ethel, Lionel and Drew. Founding father Maurice, who had been disowned by his family in England for boxing professionally, took the name Barrymore from an aging poster on an old English vaudeville house in London before leaving for America to launch his acting career.

222. Venus.

223. Tracy was paid $300,000; Oscar-winner Hepburn, $200,000.

224. $151,800.

225. Not as a Stranger, *starring Robert Mitchum as a young doctor and Olivia de Havilland as his nurse-wife.*

226. Gene Kelly. The year was 1938; the show, the Cole Porter hit Leave It to Me.

227. Sigourney Weaver.

228. What famous actor's Oscar was on display in the front window of his father's hardware store for 20 years?

229. What symbol did Charlie Chaplin wear as a parody of the swastika in his 1940 film satire *The Great Dictator*?

230. What comic strip character does Whoopi Goldberg have tattooed above her left breast?

231. Who made a cameo appearance as a man who thinks he's singer Ethel Merman in the 1980 film *Airplane!*?

232. In the 1939 film classic *The Wizard of Oz*, what did the scarecrow, played by Ray Bolger, recite to prove he had a brain?

233. What was actor Michael Keaton's name at birth?

234. What popular actress once greeted Lauren Bacall by saying, "Hi, I'm the young you"?

235. What famous Hollywood husband and wife once took out a half-page ad in *The Los Angeles Times* to deny rumors that they were splitting up?

236. What famous actress helped pay her college tuition by modeling for a brochure promoting Washington's Watergate Hotel?

228. James Stewart's. The Oscar was for his performance in the 1940 film The Philadelphia Story; the hardware store, founded by his grandfather in 1853, was in Indiana, Pennsylvania.

229. Two "x" marks—the sign of the double cross.

230. Woodstock, Snoopy's bird-buddy in the "Peanuts" comic strip.

231. Ethel Merman.

232. The Pythagorean theorum: The square of the hypotenuse of a right-angled triangle is equal to the sum of the squares of the other two sides.

233. Michael Douglas.

234. Kathleen Turner.

235. Joanne Woodward and Paul Newman. The ad cost $2,000.

236. Susan Sarandon, who at the time was known as Susan Tomalin.

237. Japanese filmmaker Akira Kurosawa's movies *The Seven Samurai* and *Yojimbo* were remade as the westerns *The Magnificent Seven* and *A Fistful of Dollars,* respectively. What American classic did his 1958 offering *The Hidden Fortress* inspire?

238. In what popular 1975 film did teenager Carrie Fisher make her screen debut?

239. Who dubbed the voice of the late Laurence Olivier when his previously cut, sexually suggestive Roman bathhouse scene with Tony Curtis was restored for the 1991 re-release of the 1960 biblical epic *Spartacus?*

240. What vehicle did Arnold Schwarzenegger receive as partial payment for starring in *Terminator 2: Judgement Day?*

241. What film star lives in a house that once served as a hideaway for gangster Al Capone?

242. What role did director John Landis have his mother, Shirley Levine, play in his 1983 Eddie Murphy-Dan Akroyd comedy *Trading Places?*

243. Who played John Wayne's young niece— orphaned, kidnapped and raised by Indians— in the great 1956 western saga *The Searchers?*

244. Who portrayed artist Paul Gauguin in *Lust for Life,* the 1956 film biography of Vincent van Gogh?

237. Star Wars, in 1977.

238. Shampoo—in which she seduces Warren Beatty.

239. Anthony Hopkins.

240. A Gulfstream G-III jet.

241. Burt Reynolds—in Jupiter, Florida.

242. A bag lady.

243. Natalie Wood.

244. Anthony Quinn, who won an Oscar as best supporting actor for his performance. Van Gogh was played by Kirk Douglas.

245. When the pedigree spaniel Lady had four puppies in the 1955 Disney film *Lady and the Tramp,* what name was given to the only one resembling papa-mutt Tramp?

246. Who was originally cast as the bumbling Inspector Jacques Clouseau before Peter Sellers got the role in the 1963 film comedy *The Pink Panther?*

247. What famous director featured his teenage daughter in a 1969 film, to the great dismay of reviewers, one of whom described her as having the face of "an exhausted gnu, the voice of an unstrung tennis racket, and a figure of no describable shape"?

248. What was the wet stuff raining down on Gene Kelly in his famous splash-dance scene in the 1952 musical *Singin' in the Rain?*

249. What was the most expensive silent film ever made?

250. What popular 1973 movie was almost renamed *Another Slow Night in Modesto* because a studio executive feared the planned title would mislead filmgoers into believing it was an Italian movie?

251. What is the only thing shown in color in Francis Ford Coppola's 1983 film *Rumble Fish?*

252. Who is the only movie star to win the best actor Academy Award two years in a row?

245. Scamp.

246. Peter Ustinov. He bowed out at the last minute.

247. John Huston—who cast his daughter, Anjelica, in a leading role in A Walk with Love and Death. *It was her film debut.*

248. A mixture of water and milk. The milk was added to make the rain more visible.

249. Ben Hur. *The 1926 epic, which starred Ramon Novarro and Francis X. Bushman, cost $3.9 million.*

250. American Graffiti.

251. Mickey Rourke's Siamese fighting fish.

252. Spencer Tracy, in 1937 and 1938, for his performances in Captains Courageous *and* Boy's Town.

253. What does R2-D2—the name of the robot in the movie *Star Wars*—mean in film editing lingo?

254. As a child, what famous actress shaved her head, wore pants and called herself "Jimmy" because she wanted to be a boy?

255. What actress, using the name Rainbo, recorded a song entitled "John, You've Gone Too Far This Time," which gently chided John Lennon for appearing nude with wife Yoko Ono on the cover of the album *Two Virgins?*

256. What was served in the 1981 film *My Dinner with Andre?*

257. In what actress's marital split was Warren Beatty named corespondent and ordered to pay the divorce costs?

258. What role did Dennis Hopper play in the 1957 western classic *The Gunfight at the O.K. Corral?*

259. What was the name of singing cowboy Gene Autry's ranch in Placerita Canyon, northwest of downtown Los Angeles?

260. Who turned down the role of the seductive and vindictive Mrs. Robinson in *The Graduate* before Anne Bancroft was offered the part in the 1967 hit film?

253. Reel 2, dialogue 2.

254. Katherine Hepburn.

255. Sissy Spacek. The record was a flop and Spacek turned her attention to acting.

256. Potato soup, fish pâté and roast quail.

257. Leslie Caron's, in 1965. British stage director Peter Hall obtained the divorce in London.

258. Billy Clanton, the youngest of the outlaw Clanton gang.

259. The Melody Ranch. Autry sold it in 1991 after the death of his horse Champion at age 41.

260. Doris Day, who explained that she rejected the part because: "I can't picture myself in bed with someone, all the crew around us, doing what I consider so exciting and exalting when it is very personal and private."

261. What popular leading man dropped out of college to tour as Snow White's Prince Charming in the *Disney on Parade* ice show?

262. How old was actor Jeff Bridges when he made his screen debut?

263. How much was producer David O. Selznick fined by the Motion Picture Association of America for letting the word "damn" be used in *Gone With the Wind?*

264. Before actor Clint Eastwood spent a record $25,000 on his winning 1986 campaign for mayor of Carmel, California, what had been the previous high for that town?

265. How many doggie spots did Walt Disney animation artists draw for the 1961 cartoon feature *One Hundred and One Dalmations?*

266. What now-famous entertainer's big break came when she jumped from the Broadway chorus of Zero Mostel's *Fiddler on the Roof* to the principal role of Tzeitel, the fiddler's eldest daughter?

267. What famous entertainer once told an interviewer, "I patterned my look after Cinderella, Mother Goose and the local hooker"?

268. What was the name of the school that murderous teenager Carrie attended in the 1976 movie shocker *Carrie?*

261. *Patrick Swayze.*

262. *Four months. He appeared as a crying baby in the 1950 film* The Company She Keeps.

263. *$5,000.*

264. *$750.*

265. *6,469,952.*

266. *Bette Midler.*

267. *Dolly Parton.*

268. *Bates High—in homage to Alfred Hitchcock and his* Psycho *killer Norman Bates.*

269. Who was originally slated to play paraplegic Vietnam War veteran Ron Kovic in the anti-war epic *Born on the Fourth of July?*

270. What does actor E.G. Marshall reply when asked what his initials stand for?

271. What leg did James Stewart have in a cast in the 1954 Alfred Hitchcock thriller *Rear Window?*

272. What famous actor won a part in the 1937 Cecil B. deMille western *The Plainsman* by pretending to be a Cheyenne Indian with little knowledge of the English language?

273. What was the name of the machine that replaced sex in Woody Allen's 1973 comedy *Sleeper?*

274. Why did *Cleopatra*, the 1963 film extravaganza starring Elizabeth Taylor, Richard Burton and Rex Harrison, have to be color-corrected before its release?

275. What did Nick and Nora Charles give their dog Asta as a Christmas present in the 1934 comedy classic *The Thin Man?*

276. When did former child screen star Shirley Temple stop believing in Santa Claus?

277. What is the French equivalent of the Oscar?

269. *Al Pacino, in 1978, but the financing fell through. The film was finally made in 1989 with Tom Cruise.*

270. *"Everyone's Guess." Marshall generally refuses to reveal his given names—but has acknowledged that the initials stand for Edda Gunther, a name that reflects his Norwegian ancestry.*

271. *Both. Most of the time, it was on the left leg. But in one scene with co-star Grace Kelly, the cast shifted to the right leg. And at the end of the movie, both legs were in casts at the same time.*

272. *Anthony Quinn, who answered a casting call for an Indian who could do a war chant in native Cheyenne.*

273. *The Orgasmatron.*

274. *Because Taylor sunbathed while outdoor scenes were being shot in Italy and her skintones in those scenes didn't match those in footage shot earlier indoors.*

275. *A toy fire hydrant.*

276. *As she tells it: "When my mother took me to see him in a department store and he asked for my autograph."*

277. *The César.*

278. In 1928, what was the only word of dialogue in MGM's first picture with sound, *White Shadows in the South Seas?*

279. What unique weapon was featured in the movies *The Tenth Victim,* starring Marcello Mastroianni and Ursula Andress, and *The Ambushers,* with Dean Martin and Janice Rule?

280. In what film did Brooke Shields make her screen debut?

281. What was Citizen Kane's full name in the 1941 Orson Welles film classic?

282. The first film documentary was screened in 1922 and given a sound track in 1939. What was it?

283. What is the "Tech" in Technicolor—the color process introduced in the Disney film *Flowers and Trees* in 1932?

284. What role did Patty Duke play in *The Miracle Worker?*

285. Leonard Slye and Frances Octavia Smith rode to fame under what show business names?

286. Who portrayed Mighty Joe Young's mistress in the movie about the giant gorilla?

278. "Hello." (It was also the first film to feature Leo the Lion's roar.)

279. A shooting bra.

280. Holy Terror, a 1977 horror movie also known as Alice, Sweet Alice.

281. Charles Foster Kane—who was modeled after publishing tycoon William Randolph Hearst.

282. The Eskimo saga Nanook of the North.

283. Inventor Herbert Kalmus' tribute to his alma mater, the Massachusetts Institute of Technology.

284. She played Helen Keller, in the 1962 movie, and Keller's teacher-companion Annie Sullivan, in the 1979 made-for-TV movie.

285. Roy Rogers and Dale Evans.

286. Terry Moore.

287. In the film *The Day the Earth Stood Still*, what words did Patricia Neal utter to stop the robot Gort from destroying the world?

288. Movie mogul Sam Goldwyn spent $20,000 to reshoot a scene in his first all-talking film, *Bulldog Drummond*, because he didn't understand what word?

289. In 1968, two movie stars won the Oscar for Best Actress. Who were they?

290. The PATSY—Picture Animal Top Star of the Year—award was first given in 1951. Who won it?

291. Who was the first actor to have a pie thrown in his face in a movie?

292. Jack Nicholson played the title role in his first movie. What was it?

293. What actress once confessed, "I used to be Snow White, but I drifted"?

294. Buddy Ebsen was originally cast as the Tin Man in the movie *The Wizard of Oz*. Why did Jack Haley replace him?

295. Where was King Kong's home?

296. Gangster Al Capone enjoyed the 1932 film *Scarface* so much that he gave director Howard Hawkes a gift. What was it?

287. *Klaatu barada nikto.*

288. *"Din." He had it changed to "noise".*

289. *Katherine Hepburn, for* The Lion in Winter, *and Barbra Streisand, for* Funny Girl.

290. *Francis the Talking Mule.*

291. *Cross-eyed comic Ben Turpin, in an early Keystone Kop film. Mabel Normand threw it.*

292. The Crybaby Killer, *in 1958.*

293. *Mae West.*

294. *Ebsen's aluminum-dust makeup turned him bright blue and sent him to the hospital with serious respiratory problems. Different makeup was devised for Haley.*

295. *Skull Island.*

296. *A miniature machine gun.*

297. In what movie did long-time Superman George Reeves make his screen debut?

298. In the saucy 1953 comedy *The Moon is Blue*, starring William Holden, David Niven, and Maggie McNamara, what word made its movie debut and caused the film to be banned in several parts of the country?

299. To whom did actor Ryan O'Neal mail a live tarantula?

300. What was the name of the general played by Sterling Hayden in the movie *Dr. Strangelove?*

301. Who played the title role in *Marty* when it was presented as a TV movie in 1953—three years before the Oscar-winning film starring Ernest Borgnine?

302. Who starred in: *The Black Camel, Black Dragons, Black Friday, The Black Sheep,* and two films entitled *The Black Cat?*

303. In the movie *Bananas,* who did the play-by-play on Woody Allen's wedding night with Louise Lasser?

304. What British actress made her stage debut at age 33, when she appeared as a fairy with a long nose in a pantomime play called *Little Jack Horner?*

305. What was the name of the sewer worker attacked by a 36-foot alligator in the 1980 monster movie, *Alligator?*

297. Gone With the Wind. He played Brent Tarleton, one of the redheaded twins who wooed Scarlett O'Hara.

298. "Virgin."

299. Gossip commentator Rona Barrett.

300. Gen. Jack D. Ripper.

301. Rod Steiger.

302. Bela Lugosi.

303. Sportscaster Howard Cosell.

304. Margaret Rutherford, who was 71 when she made her first Miss Marple movie and 80 when she died.

305. Ed Norton, undoubtedly in deference to the character created by Art Carney in TV's The Honeymooners.

306. Where did John Wayne get his nickname Duke?

307. Who portrayed the dying sea captain who delivered the *Maltese Falcon* in the 1941 John Huston film classic?

308. What actor started his career on Broadway in 1922 as one of the robots in Karel Capek's *R.U.R.?*

309. What foreign actress once earned a living as a model, working under the name Diana Loris?

310. What actress once said, "Sometimes I'm so sweet, even I can't stand it"?

311. Who played wise-guy dragster Bob Falfa in the movie *American Graffiti?*

312. There were 291 words spoken in *The Jazz Singer*, the first motion picture feature with a sound track. What six are the most famous?

313. What two people involved in the 1956 movie *The Invasion of the Body Snatchers* had cameo roles in the 1978 remake?

314. What actress had a daughter by Marcello Mastroianni and a son by Roger Vadim but married neither of them?

315. How did HAL, the computer in *2001: A Space Odyssey*, get its name?

306. From his favorite childhood dog, an Airedale called Duke.

307. John Huston's actor-father, Walter.

308. Spencer Tracy.

309. Gina Lollobrigida.

310. Julie Andrews.

311. Harrison Ford.

312. Al Jolson's first: "You ain't heard nothing yet, folks!"

313. Star Kevin McCarthy and director Don Siegel.

314. Catherine Deneuve.

315. Advance each letter by one and you have the answer—IBM.

316. What country was 'The Mouse That Roared' in the Peter Sellers movie of that name?

317. Who played the ancient lama in the 1937 movie *Lost Horizon?*

318. What actress performed topless in Las Vegas before breaking into the movies as an outer space sex siren?

319. Robert Mitchum launched his film career playing bad guy bit parts in whose cowboy movies?

320. What actor first went to Hollywood as a chaperone-bodyguard for a gangster's girlfriend?

321. Who made her film debut in the 1948 film *Scudda-Hoo! Scudda-Hay!?*

322. What two Brooklyn comedians named Kaminsky gained fame under other names?

323. When Janet Gaynor won the first Academy Award for Best Actress in 1928, who won for Best Actor?

324. What actor has to cover his arm with make-up when he performs in order to mask tattoos proclaiming his love for Mom and Dad and Scotland?

325. Where was Francis Ford Coppola's Vietnam epic *Apocalypse Now* filmed?

316. The Grand Duchy of Fenwick.

317. Sam Jaffe.

318. Valerie Perrine. Her film debut was as Montana Wildhack in Slaughterhouse Five.

319. Hopalong Cassidy's.

320. George Raft, who watched over nightclub singer Texas Guinan for his buddy Owney "the Killer" Madden.

321. Marilyn Monroe. She was in the distant background rowing a boat.

322. David Daniel Kaminsky, who became Danny Kaye; and Melvin Kaminsky, who became Mel Brooks. They are not related.

323. Emil Jannings.

324. Sean Connery, best known for his James Bond portrayal.

325. In the Philippines.

326. Who played Humpty Dumpty in the 1933 movie *Alice in Wonderland?*

327. In what 1968 film did Marlon Brando play a long-haired Jewish guru; Ringo Starr, a Mexican gardener; Charles Aznavour, a hunchback; and Richard Burton, an alcoholic Welsh poet?

328. What famous comedian played the Tin Woodman in the 1925 silent-movie version of *The Wizard of Oz?*

329. Who was the first black performer signed to a long-term contract by a major Hollywood studio?

330. Where did the Warner Brothers—Jack, Harry, Sam and Albert—get the 99 chairs they used in the first theater they opened in 1903 in New Castle, Pennsylvania?

331. Where was Anthony "Zorba the Greek" Quinn born?

332. Whose ashes does actor Marlon Brando keep in his home in Tahiti?

333. What was the name of Hollywood's first 3-D movie, released in 1952?

334. Who portrayed Mia Farrow's sister in Woody Allen's *Zelig* and *The Purple Rose of Cairo?*

326. W.C. Fields.

327. Candy, *based on Terry Southern's novel.*

328. Oliver Hardy, *of Laurel and Hardy fame.*

329. *Singer Lena Horne, in 1942. The studio was Metro-Goldwyn-Mayer.*

330. *From the local undertaker. The chairs had to be returned whenever there was a funeral.*

331. *In Chihuahua, Mexico.*

332. *Those of his childhood friend, comedian Wally Cox, who died in 1973.*

333. Bwana Devil.

334. *Mia's sister, Stephanie Farrow.*

335. What famous funnyman co-authored the 1974 film comedy *Blazing Saddles* with actor-director Mel Brooks?

336. In what film did actress Dorothy Lamour first don a sarong?

337. What famous leading man turned down the role of Rhett Butler in *Gone With the Wind* and predicted it would be "the biggest flop in Hollywood history"?

338. On what day of the week was actress Tuesday Weld born?

339. Which two top Hollywood stars turned down the role of Professor Henry Higgins in the film version of *My Fair Lady* before Rex Harrison was offered the part?

340. From what earlier stage name did actress-comedienne Whoopi Goldberg derive her current name?

341. What two Frank Sinatra movie thrillers did Ole Blue Eyes own and order shelved for years because of their frightening political themes?

342. Who played Robert Redford's laid-back rodeo pal and manager in the 1979 film *The Electric Horseman?*

335. Richard Pryor.

336. In her very first movie, The Jungle Princess, *in 1936—four years before her first "Road" movie with Bob Hope and Bing Crosby.*

337. Gary Cooper.

338. Friday—August 27, 1943.

339. Cary Grant and James Cagney.

340. Whoopi Cushion.

341. The Manchurian Candidate, *made in 1962, and* Suddenly, *made in 1954—both of which dealt with political assassinations.*

342. Country singer Willie Nelson.

343. What actor was dropped by Universal Studios in the early 1950s because of his protruding Adam's apple and slow speech?

344. What star—seven months pregnant with her first child—sang the Oscar-winning song "Once I Had a Secret Love" at the 1953 Academy Awards show?

345. Ronald Reagan used a famous line from one of his movies as the title of his 1965 autobiography. What's the line?

346. The family name of what famous fictional sleuth was Charalambides before it was anglicized by an immigration official on Ellis Island?

347. What unusual stipulation was included in funnyman Buster Keaton's contract with MGM?

348. What song does Kate Capshaw sing in broken Chinese in the opening scene of the 1984 film *Indiana Jones and the Temple of Doom?*

349. Robert Redford turned down the lead role in *The Graduate* because he considered himself too old. How old was Dustin Hoffman when he took the part?

350. The mother of what famous European actress once won a Great Garbo look-alike contest and a trip to Hollywood to work as Garbo's double?

351. What actress changed her name to avoid seeking fame and fortune as Sarah Jane Fulks?

343. Clint Eastwood.

344. Ann Blyth sang the song, which was from the movie Calamity Jane.

345. "Where's the rest of me?"—words he delivered in the 1941 film King's Row when he woke up and discovered both his legs had been amputated.

346. "The Thin Man" Nick Charles.

347. He was not to smile in public.

348. The Cole Porter classic "Anything Goes."

349. Thirty—the same age as Redford.

350. Sophia Loren. But her mother never made the trip because her own mother (Sophia's grandmother) wouldn't let her.

351. Jane Wyman.